Israel, Iran, ISIS
in Bible Prophecy

Israel, Iran, ISIS in Bible Prophecy

Greg Laurie

Israel, Iran, ISIS in Bible Prophecy

Contents

Israel, Iran, and ISIS in Bible Prophecy

Introduction

A new poll reveals that Americans believe our country has spun off of its axis and is out of control. But let me take it a step further. It is not the United States that is out of control; it's the entire world. Why? It's because we are living in the last days.

The Bible tells us in 2 Timothy 3 that in the last days, things will go from bad to worse. We could compare last days events to dominoes that are closely stacked together. Once the first domino goes, the others will fall in rapid succession.

That is how it will be with world events in the last days, beginning with the emergence of the Antichrist. Then there is the Tribulation period. Then there is the Battle of Armageddon. Then there is the Second Coming of Jesus Christ. Then there is the Millennium. These events are closely stacked together. And once the first one starts, the others will follow in rapid succession. Events in our world today are getting very close to that. I think I can safely say that we have never been closer to the return of Jesus than we are right now.

A while back I did a radio interview, where I was a guest along with a college professor who was challenging my belief that Christ was coming back.

I told him, "Well, sir, I believe that you are actually a fulfillment of Bible prophecy." I don't think he had ever heard that before.

He said, "Well, why would you think that?"

So I read him this verse from 2 Peter 3: "Most importantly, I want to remind you that in the last days scoffers will come, mocking the truth and following their own desires. They will say, 'What happened to the promise that Jesus is coming again? From before the times of our ancestors, everything has remained the same since the world was first created' " (verses 3–4 NLT).

This has been the argument: We have heard all this before.

But there have been things that have happened and are happening right now that should be of great interest to the Bible student. What is significant today is the cumulative effect, the convergence of so many more signs at one time, which cause me to wonder whether we are the generation that will see Jesus return.

The Bible says that we should be looking for an increase in frequency of these signs, like that of a woman who is getting ready to go into labor. We are told in 1 Thessalonians 5:3–4, "For when they say, 'Peace and safety!' then sudden destruction comes upon them, as labor pains upon a pregnant woman. And they shall not escape. But you, brethren, are not in darkness, so that this Day should overtake you as a thief."

Jesus Christ is coming back again. That is clearly taught in the Bible, and no Bible-believing Christian would ever dispute that truth.

One-third of the Bible deals with the topic of prophecy or end times events. This is important to God, and therefore it should be important to us. In addition, the Bible deals with the subject of the return of Christ five times more frequently than any other topic. Therefore, because Jesus came the first time, we can be sure He will come the second time.

When you think about it, our lives are governed by signs. From the moment we get up in the morning, we are looking at signs. We see them on our computer screens. We see them as we are driving. We see them in buildings. We see them at sporting events. The list goes on and on, and so do the signs of the times.

We want to pay attention to the signs of the times that are all around us, reminding us of the fact that the return of Jesus is near. They are telling us that we could be hurtled into eternity in a moment, in the twinkling of an eye.

My prayer is that every one of us would be living in a way that is pleasing to the Lord as we prepare ourselves for His return. I also pray that anyone reading these words who does not yet know Jesus would believe in Him so they can be ready to meet Him in Heaven one day.

1

A New World Order?

In October 2014, at the Aspen Institute's Washington Ideas Forum, Former United States Defense Secretary Chuck Hagel was quoted as saying, "I think we are living through one of these historic, defining times. I think we are seeing a new world order."

Hagel went on to say, "What we're seeing in the Middle East with ISIL is going to require a steady, long-term effort. It's going to require coalitions of common interests, which we are forming."[1]

We have shifting and change in global powers right now. A new world order will emerge. And I believe there are things happening right now that we have never seen before in human history. It is a reminder that Christ is coming.

To begin with, there is the modern state of Israel. The Bible clearly has said that the Jews would be scattered and then regathered in their homeland once again. In fact, Jesus warned that the temple would be dismantled and that judgment would come upon the city of Jerusalem. And surely judgment came.

In AD 70, the Roman conqueror Titus rolled into Jerusalem with his forces and captured the city. The Jewish people were scattered around the world. Then, during World War II, six million Jews were murdered in Nazi death camps such as Auschwitz, Dachau, and Ravensbrück. Yet after the Holocaust, the Jews began to return to their homeland. And only a few years after World War II ended, they had formed a nation. On May 14, 1948, the modern State of Israel was declared, and the prophetic time clock began to tick.

Who would have thought that the Jewish people would manage to return to their homeland and form a nation once again? It's unprecedented. Never before has a nation of people been able to maintain their national unity or identity three to five hundred years after being removed from their homeland. Yet that is what happened with Israel. This is not only a sign of the end times, but it's what we would call a supersign.

Not only did the Bible prophesy that the Jewish people would return to their homeland, but it also predicts that Israel would have control of the city of Jerusalem. Yet when Israel became a nation again on May 14, 1948, that was not the case. Jerusalem actually was under control of the Kingdom of Jordan. But in 1967, during the Six-Day War, Israeli forces, after being attacked, went in and recaptured Jerusalem. And for the first time in two thousand years, Jerusalem came under the control of the Jewish people once again. The Scriptures clearly teach that Jerusalem will be at the epicenter of end times events.

Today, Jerusalem remains at the heart of the Israeli-Palestinian conflict. Many Arab leaders insist that Jerusalem and the entire West Bank are rightfully Palestinian territory. As a condition for peace, they say that it must be given back. The Palestinian people want the West Bank, and they want Jerusalem.

Not only that, they will not acknowledge the right of Israel to exist. Do you think you could have a meaningful relationship with someone who refused to acknowledge your right to exist? That is what the Jewish people are facing right now. And that is why the conflict continues and peace talks continue to break down.

Then there is Islamic terrorism. It seems like every time we turn around, there is a new terrorist attack. There was one in Afghanistan recently, where a suicide bomber exploded himself. At the time of this writing, ISIS carries out regular acts of unspeakable violence and atrocity, including beheadings, rapes, and burning a man alive. ISIS is now recruiting children as young as age nine, dubbed the "Cubs of the Caliphate," to train them in terrorist activities. This has gotten so bad that the United Nations now says that ISIS is guilty of war crimes.

Then there is the terror group Boko Haram, which has killed thousands of people and has abducted hundreds of women and children. According to Human Rights Watch, the group has abducted at least five hundred women and girls since mid-2013.[2]

Then there was the November 2014 attack on a Jerusalem synagogue, where two Palestinians armed with meat cleavers, knives, and a handgun killed four men, with a fifth victim, a police officer, later dying of his wounds. Three of those murdered were rabbis from the United States. Meanwhile, news of the attack was greeted with celebration and dancing in the streets in the West Bank.

These attackers all have one thing in common: they are Islamic. I am not saying that every Muslim is a terrorist, because clearly that is not the case. But I am saying that all of these terror groups are Islamic. They have many names, such as Al-Qaeda, ISIS, Hamas, Hezbollah, and Boko Haram. This is what we are dealing with in our world today, and it's only getting worse.

Curiously, and as a cause of some concern, we do not find the reigning superpower, the United States, in the Bible's last days prophetic scenario. People who are powerful today will not be during that time. A new world order is going to appear, and there will be the emergence of Antichrist and his confederation of ten nations in this new world order.

Think about It

- As terms like "new world order" enter into our public discussions more frequently, how do you feel about the future? Are you fearful? Optimistic? None of the above? Explain your answer.

- If you are a believer, what perspective could you share with a nonbeliever in a discussion about Israel, her fairly recent establishment as a nation, her role in the Middle East, and a new world order? What Scripture passages might you use to make your point? Jot down the references here.

- Look up Isaiah 26:3. In light of current events, how does this verse encourage you? What would you say to someone who is feeling fearful about the world's state of affairs?

Greg Laurie

2

What the Bible Predicts about Israel

It's amazing that one little city can create such a stir. It won't be Paris taking center stage in end times events . . . or Rome . . . or London . . . or Los Angeles . . . or even New York City. No, it will be the forty-nine-square-mile city of Jerusalem, the capital of Israel.

But why? What's behind this hostility? We find the answer in Zechariah 12, where God says, "I will make Jerusalem like an intoxicating drink that makes the nearby nations stagger when they send their armies to besiege Jerusalem and Judah. On that day I will make Jerusalem an immovable rock. All the nations will gather against it to try to move it, but they will only hurt themselves" (verses 2–3 NLT). God was saying that in the last days, Jerusalem will be a burdensome stone. And that's exactly what it is today.

Anti-Semitism, at its very roots, is Satanic. We can trace this back to the first Messianic passage in the book of Genesis. Here God drew the battle lines and said to Satan, "And I will put enmity between you and the woman, and between your seed and her Seed; He shall bruise your head, and you shall bruise His heel" (Genesis 3:15). From that point on, we can follow the story through the Scriptures. In Exodus, we see the Pharaoh trying to kill the Hebrew baby boys (Moses, of course, survived). In the book of Esther, we find the attempt by Haman to annihilate the Jewish people—sort of a forerunner of the Final Solution, as Hitler called his plan. In the New Testament, we read of Herod killing the Jewish baby boys, trying to eradicate the Messiah. So we see that hatred against God's chosen people, the Jewish people, comes from the Devil himself.

Dr. John F. Walvoord, a respected expert on Bible prophecy, said, "The prophecies about Jerusalem make it clear that the Holy City will be in the center of world events in the end time. . . . The conflict between Israel and the Palestinian Arabs will focus more and more attention on Jerusalem. . . . In all of these situations Jerusalem is the city to watch, as the city of prophetic destiny prepares to act out her final role."[3]

God gave the land of Israel to the Jewish people. This is clear in the Scriptures. God said to Israel, "Look, I am giving all this land to you! Go in and occupy it, for it is the land the Lord swore to give to your ancestors Abraham, Isaac, and Jacob, and to all their descendants" (Deuteronomy 1:8 NLT). This is the land that God gave to the Jewish people, and they have returned to their homeland.

Then, over in Ezekiel 37, God speaks of Israel's being scattered and then brought back to life:

> The LORD took hold of me, and I was carried away by the Spirit of the LORD to a valley filled with bones. He led me all around among the bones that covered the valley floor. They were scattered everywhere across the ground and were completely dried out. Then he asked me, "Son of man, can these bones become living people again?"
>
> "O Sovereign LORD," I replied, "you alone know the answer to that."

Then he said to me, "Speak a prophetic message to these bones and say, 'Dry bones, listen to the word of the LORD! This is what the Sovereign LORD says: Look! I am going to put breath into you and make you live again! I will put flesh and muscles on you and cover you with skin. I will put breath into you, and you will come to life. Then you will know that I am the LORD.'" (verses 1–6 NLT)

Essentially God took Ezekiel to a cemetery and said, "Preach to the people in the graves." (I've spoken to some dead audiences before, but this takes the cake.)

Whom do these bones represent? We find the answer in verses 11–14:

Then he said to me, "Son of man, these bones represent the people of Israel. They are saying, 'We have become old, dry bones—all hope is gone. Our nation is finished.' Therefore, prophesy to them and say, 'This is what the Sovereign LORD says: O my people, I will open your graves of exile and cause you to rise again. Then I will bring you back to the land of Israel. When this happens, O my people, you will know that I am the LORD. I will put my Spirit in you, and you will live again and return home to your own land. Then you will know that I, the LORD, have spoken, and I have done what I said. Yes, the LORD has spoken!'"

Is that clear enough? God has broken this down in a way we can understand. Israel was being scattered, then they would be regathered and return to their homeland. And that is exactly where we are today.

Not only that, but after Ezekiel 37 speaks of the people of Israel being scattered and brought back to life, Ezekiel 38 says that a large nation to the north of Israel's newly established homeland, along with a number of allies, will invade Israel from every direction:

> This is another message that came to me from the LORD: "Son of man, turn and face Gog of the land of Magog, the prince who rules over the nations of Meshech and Tubal, and prophesy against him. . . . I will turn you around and put hooks in your jaws to lead you out with your whole army—your horses and charioteers in full armor and a great horde armed with shields and swords. Persia, Ethiopia, and Libya will join you, too, with all their weapons. Gomer and all its armies will also join you, along with the armies of Beth-togarmah from the distant north, and many others." (verses 1–2, 4–6 NLT)

The Bible is very clear in saying that this is a specific event of the last days. God was saying this is in the future—the distant future:

> "A long time from now you will be called into action. In the distant future you will swoop down

on the land of Israel, which will be enjoying peace
after recovering from war and after its people
have returned from many lands to the mountains
of Israel." (verse 8 NLT)

The passage goes on to say,

"This is what the Sovereign LORD says: At that
time evil thoughts will come to your mind, and
you will devise a wicked scheme. You will say,
'Israel is an unprotected land filled with unwalled
villages! I will march against her and destroy
these people who live in such confidence!' "
(verses 10–11 NLT)

These people who live in such confidence . . . That is an interesting phrase. Really, it's an unthinkable phrase concerning Israel at any time in her history—until now. Certainly this couldn't have been said after the Holocaust, or after Israel had declared its statehood, or after the Six-Day War in 1967, or after the Yom Kippur War in 1973. Israel still could have been defeated. But the Israel of today is much different than the Israel of yesterday. Today the military of Israel is greatly respected. In fact, because of Israel's military prowess, intelligence, and possession of nuclear weapons, the other nations know that when Israel says they will do something, they will do it. Relatively speaking, Israel is living in confidence today.

So as we look at the Bible's prophecies concerning Israel, we see that a number of significant things have already happened.

The Bible says that Israel would be scattered. Check. This happened in AD 70, when Titus conquered Jerusalem.

The Bible says that Israel would be regathered. Check. This happened on May 14, 1948, when the State of Israel was declared.

The Bible says that Israel would regain Jerusalem. Check. This happened in 1967, during the Six-Day War.

The Bible says that in the last days, Israel will be isolated from the other nations of the world. We need to look no further than current headlines to see this is happening today.

The Bible says that after Israel has regathered as a nation, it would be attacked by a large force to her north. This has not happened yet. But it could at any time.

Think about It

- In Deuteronomy 1:8 God said, "Look, I am giving all this land to you! Go in and occupy it, for it is the land the Lord swore to give to your ancestors Abraham, Isaac, and Jacob, and to all their descendants" (NLT). Using a Bible concordance, what other verses can you find that indicate God has given this land to the Jewish people?

- Based on your own recollection of current events or by doing a search of Internet news sites, how do you see Israel becoming increasingly isolated from other nations of the world?

- Take a few moments to skim Ezekiel 37–39. What verses

about Israel especially stand out to you? How do they help you in your understanding of Israel's history and her role in the last days?

- Psalm 122:6–7 says, "Pray for the peace of Jerusalem: 'May they prosper who love you. Peace be within your walls, prosperity within your palaces.' " What does this verse mean to you? How will you pray for Israel today?

_____

_____

_____

_____

_____

_____

_____

_____

_____

_____

_____

_____

_____

_____

_____

_____

_____

3

Other Nations in the End Times

Get out a map of the world and find the little sliver of land in the Middle East known as Israel. Now look to Israel's north. What do you find? You find Russia. Is Russia actually the force known as Magog, which the Bible says will march against Israel in the last days? No one can say with absolute certainty, but I think we can make a pretty good case for it.

Magog was the second son of Japheth (see Genesis 10:2), whose descendants, according to the Jewish historian Josephus, settled north of the Black Sea. The descendants of Tubal and Meshech, Japheth's fifth and six sons, settled south of the Black Sea. These tribes intermarried and became known as Magog, settling to the north of Israel. In Ezekiel 39, God says, "I am your enemy, O Gog, ruler of the nations of Meshech and Tubal. I will turn you around and drive you toward the mountains of Israel, bringing you from the distant north" (verses 1–2 NLT).

Then there are the allies that ultimately will march with Magog. In Ezekiel 38 God says to Gog, "Persia, Ethiopia, and Libya will join you, too, with all their weapons" (verse 5 NLT). Persia officially became known as Iran in 1935. If you were to meet people from Iran today, they might even identify themselves as Persian, because that is their heritage. And in 1979, Iran became an Islamic republic.

If the Magog that Ezekiel is speaking of is indeed Russia, then it's fascinating that Iran is identified as an ally of Magog's. It is worth noting that for 2,500 years, Russia had no alliance with Persia (Iran). That is, until now. Today they are officially allies, and Russia has signed a billion-dollar deal to sell weapons to Iran.[4] An alliance prophesied 2,500 years ago has been formed now. It is indeed a sign of the times.

In addition to its alliance with Russia, Iran recently has formed an alliance with North Korea. A member of the US State Department has said, "Iran declared Sept. 1, 2012 North Korea was part of their 'Axis of Resistance,' which only includes Iran, Syria, and Hezbollah. They've announced to the world they are essentially allies with North Korea."[5] Clearly a rogue nation, North Korea has been developing nuclear weapons and has even fired off missiles.

The United States has been negotiating with Iran over nuclear weapons, under the assumption that Iran's leadership is more moderate today than in the past. We remember Mahmoud Ahmadinejad, Iran's former president, and his inflammatory rhetoric. Now there is a so-called moderate leader of Iran. Yet we still hear statements from Iran about wanting to wipe Israel off the map. General Mohammad Naghdi, commander of Iran's Basij forces, recently stated, "Our ideal is not [nuclear] centrifuges but the destruction of the White House and the annihilation of Zionism [Israel]."[6]

Some may pass these off as empty threats. But are they? Remember, threats of this nature against the Jewish people also came from Nazi Germany. And had it not been for US intervention during World War II, who knows how many more Jewish people would have been murdered? So when Israel hears someone say they want to wipe their nation off the face of the earth, they take it seriously. So they should. As Israel's Prime Minister Benjamin Netanyahu has said, "There is no moderation in Iran. It is unrepentant, unreformed. It calls for Israel's eradication. It promotes international terrorism."[7] Prime Minister Netanyahu also stated in his March 3, 2015, address to Congress that "to defeat ISIS and let Iran get nuclear weapons would be to win the battle, but lose the war. We can't let that happen."[8]

Which brings us to ISIS (or ISIL, the Islamic State of Iraq and the Levant). Initially dismissed as a junior varsity rebel group, they are ready for prime time. What is unusual about them is they are a terrorist army, and we have never faced a terrorist army before. According to the United Nations, ISIS has stored a massive amount of weapons. The group has captured vehicles, missiles, rockets, rocket launchers, anti-aircraft guns, two varieties of tanks, and ammo sufficient to equip more than three Iraqi conventional army divisions.

Not only that, but ISIS is well funded. They make up to $2 million per day off black market crude oil sales from captured regions.[9] They also produce millions of dollars through ransom payments, extortion, and profits from the people they capture and sell as sex slaves.

Originally ISIS was what we might call a competitor with Al-Qaeda. But they have recently formed a pact to work together, which isn't good news for the rest of the world. They use social media and have managed to attract certain people from the United Kingdom and even the United States to their cause.

We see forces like this developing, and we wonder what it all means. We wonder where the United States is in all of this. As we look at the nations of the world that have raised their hand against Israel and tried to wipe her out—and the list is long—we see that God dealt with them. Yet historically, the United States has stood as a staunch ally of Israel.

When Israel declared her statehood in 1948, the United States was the first to acknowledge her. In some ways, however, I think the United States needs Israel more than Israel needs the United States. I base that on God's statement to Abraham when He said, "I will bless those who bless you, and I will curse him who curses you; and in you all the families of the earth shall be blessed" (Genesis 12:3). I believe one of the reasons God has blessed the United States is because of our continued support for the Jewish people and their homeland.

But now the United States finds itself in a precarious and unusual position of not standing by Israel as closely as we have in the past. I hope that is rectified. Let's pray that the Lord will direct our leaders and our president to understand that we don't just support Israel because it is the only true democracy in the Middle East, but because Israel is our ally, our friend. They are God's chosen people, placed there in that land by God Himself.

We don't know where the United States of America is in the prophetic scenario of the last days, and that concerns me. How could a nation of our size not be mentioned? I could offer a number of ideas as to why this may be, but here are a few.

Perhaps the United States will fall in line with other nations and be a part of the confederacy of the Antichrist.

It could be the United States is absent from the end times scenario because of an economic collapse in our nation or because the United States will be in some kind of a war or nuclear conflict.

But my favorite option is this one. If even half the Americans who claim to be Christians really are believers, it means that when the rapture of the church takes place, so many Americans would be caught up to meet the Lord that our country would essentially collapse overnight. Think about it. If in our nation of some 318 million today, people in government, the military, the medical field, and in every other field you can think of were to suddenly disappear, what would happen to our nation? What would happen if people in all those areas were to simultaneously disappear? You could see how the United States would diminish as a world power.

Yet here is an interesting twist on the narrative. The Bible says that in the last days, Israel not only will regather as a nation, but she also will be isolated. She won't have an ally like the United States standing with her. According to the Scriptures, it is only a matter of time until Israel will stand alone.

Why will God allow this? Because when Magog, the large force from the north, attacks her, God says that He will step in. We read in Ezekiel 38,

> "But this is what the Sovereign LORD says: When Gog invades the land of Israel, my fury will boil over! In my jealousy and blazing anger, I promise a mighty shaking in the land of Israel on that day. . . . I will punish you and your armies with disease and bloodshed; I will send torrential rain, hailstones, fire, and burning sulfur! In this way, I will show my greatness and holiness, and I will make myself known to all the nations of the world. Then they will know that I am the LORD." (verses 18–19, 22–23 NLT)

The Lord will decimate the armies of Magog and her allies, and it will take seven years for them to burn the weapons from that conflict (see Ezekiel 39:9). Then God says, "And I will never again turn my face from [my people], for I will pour out my Spirit upon the people of Israel" (verse 29 NLT).

So is Russia Magog? Maybe. I don't know for certain. But I do know this much. The Bible says that in the last days, Iran will have a role to play, and Israel will have a role to play. And it's most likely that Russia will have a role to play as well.

Think about It

• Do you think Russia is the modern-day Magog that the Bible speaks of? Why or why not? Explain your answer.

• Why do you think the United States is absent from the Bible's prophecies concerning the last days? In light of this, what do you think should be the priorities for Christians and churches in the United States today? In what ways can they make a difference in their communities? In the workplace? In their schools? In their families?

• Do you think it's important for Christians to be aware of and well-versed in current events? Why or why not?

• How might a Christian use a discussion of current events to build a bridge for sharing the gospel? Give some examples.

• In what ways has this chapter challenged or changed your thinking regarding current events? How could you pray for your own nation today?

4

Are You Ready for Christ's Return?

My friend Skip Heitzig tells the story about a little town he visited a while ago called Wall, in South Dakota. In this town, which has a population of around 700, there is a store called Wall Drug, started by a pharmacist named Ted Hustead. Mr. Hustead knew that he wouldn't be able to generate that much business in a small town, so he decided to publicize his drugstore around the country—and actually around the world. He put up signs for his store everywhere, telling people how far they were from Wall Drug. For instance, in Memphis, Tennessee, you will see a sign that says WALL DRUG, 1,192 MILES. A sign in Paris, France, reads WALL DRUG, 5,961 MILES. Signs for Wall Drug can be found in Russia, Kenya, and even in India. On Interstate 90 in South Dakota, you will find 53 signs in the last 45 minutes before you reach Wall Drug. And as you make your way closer and closer, the signs get bigger and brighter.

Jesus told us to be aware of the signs of His return. And when those signs get closer together and bigger and brighter, we know that His coming is near. In fact, it seems as though every time we turn around, there is a new sign. That is what Jesus said it would be like before His return. These events will be happening closer and closer together, and we certainly are seeing that today.

But for those of us who are believers, here is where it gets teresting. As I mentioned earlier, God will pour out His Spirit on the people of Israel (see Ezekiel 39:29). But before this takes place, God's work with the non-Jews must come to a crescendo. The apostle Paul wrote, "For I do not desire, brethren, that you should be ignorant of this mystery, lest you should be wise in your own opinion, that blindness in part has happened to Israel until the fullness of the Gentiles has come in" (Romans 11:25).

Until the fullness of the Gentiles has come in . . . What does this mean? I am a Gentile, not a Jew, and I have been grafted into the promises of Abraham, Isaac, and Jacob, as most of us as Christians have (see Romans 11:17–20). When God is done with us, and we are caught up to meet the Lord in the air, then God will pour out His Spirit on the Jewish people.

Largely across our world today, Jewish people are resistant to the gospel. Of course, there are Jewish Christians who love the Lord and who call Jesus their Messiah, their *Yeshua Hamashiach*. But there is coming a day when the eyes of many Jewish people will be opened. This will be sparked by God's intervention in saving Israel from the attack of Magog and its allies.

So as I see world events unfolding as they are, I wonder if perhaps the Lord isn't waiting for that last person to believe before He calls His church home. In fact, he or she may be walking around on Earth somewhere today. Can you imagine if you knew who this person was? You would want to apply a little pressure, wouldn't you?

"Let's just pray, and if you want to accept Christ, pray this now: 'Lord Jesus, come into my life.' "

Then *boom!* Just like that, it happens. We're caught up to meet the Lord in the air.

That day will come. We don't know when. But we can certainly see the signs of the times.

My question for you is are you ready? If Jesus were to come back today, would you be caught up to meet Him in the air, or would you be left behind?

Not long ago I read a news article about ISIS militants who stoned a woman to death for adultery. These militants, along with the girl's father, put her into a hole they had dug in the ground and then stoned her to death for committing this crime. Because the girl's father was the "most humiliated," he was given the highest honor of throwing the biggest stone at his daughter as she pled for her life. As she begged him for forgiveness, her father coldly replied, "I am not your father anymore."[10]

This reminds me of another story: the woman who had been caught in the act of adultery and was thrown before Jesus. Her accusers weren't ISIS militants; they were religious Pharisees. They said to Jesus, "Teacher, this woman was caught in adultery, in the very act. Now Moses, in the law, commanded us that such should be stoned. But what do You say?" (John 8:4–5).

So Jesus did the most amazing thing. He stooped down and began to write on the ground. Then He stood up, faced the crowd, and said, "He who is without sin among you, let him throw a stone at her first" (verse 7).

The Bible says that one by one they left, from the eldest to the youngest. I wonder what Jesus wrote on the ground that day. No one knows with any certainty. But I will give you my opinion. I think what He wrote on the ground were the names of the woman's accusers. Maybe he looked up at the crowd and then traced a name in the dirt. *Caleb . . . got your name here. Morde-cai . . . your name is here. Abraham . . . Joshua . . . your names are here too.* And next to their names, maybe He wrote what their secret sin was. On and on it went until Jesus had cleared the room, and the woman was left alone with Jesus.

Then He said to her, "Woman, where are those accusers of yours? Has no one condemned you?" (verse 10).

She said, "No one, Lord."

Jesus told her, "Neither do I condemn you; go and sin no more" (verse 11).

Was Jesus simply turning a blind eye to this woman's sin? I don't think so. She knew she was a sinner. She knew she was guilty. But she had believed in Jesus at this point and had already turned to Him.

How do we know that?

Notice that in answer to His question, she called Him Lord. And that is how long it takes to believe in Jesus. In an instant.

And here's something interesting. Note how Jesus addressed her. He said in verse 10, "Woman, where are those accusers of yours? Has no one condemned you?"

The word Jesus used for *woman* was not what she was expecting. It could be translated "Ma'am" or "Lady." It was a term of respect, the same Hebrew word Jesus used to address His own mother when He hung on the cross. It's a word you would use to speak to an older woman or a woman whom you respect.

I'm sure this woman had been called a lot of things in her life, but probably never *Ma'am* or *Lady*. But Jesus didn't simply see her for what she was. He saw her for what she would become.

And that is how He sees you. You may look at your life today and see failure or weakness or sin. God looks at your life and sees that too. But He also sees what He can make you into.

Unlike the father who refused to listen to his daughter's cries for forgiveness, God hears our prayers. When we say, "Father, forgive us," He listens and answers because of the death of Jesus on the cross. He died for our sins so that we could be forgiven.

Maybe you are in some kind of sin right now. Maybe it is the sin of adultery, or maybe it is another sin. Whatever sin it is, God will forgive you today if you will turn from it and put your faith in Him.

One thing we all want to be sure of is that we are ready to meet the Lord. I believe we are living in the last days. But even if we are not as far along on the Bible's prophetic calendar as I believe we are, I know this much: in your life, you may be in your last days.

Some of us are older, so it's obvious that we're in our last days. But there are others who are younger who could be in their last days, too.

"I'm thirty," someone might say. "I have at least thirty more years, minimum."

Maybe. Or maybe not. Maybe it's five years. Maybe it's two years. Or maybe it's less. No one knows. You don't know when God will bring your life to an end. That is why the Bible says, "Prepare to meet your God" (Amos 4:12).

God has given you life, a precious commodity. Every day it is deposited into your account to use or neglect. Use it well.

This may be one of your last opportunities to get right with God. Jesus is coming. Life is short. Don't put it off until later. Do it now. Make sure you are ready to meet the Lord.

Think about It

- If Christ were to return or if you were to die today, would you be ready? How do you know for certain that you are right with God?

- What would you say to those who don't believe that Jesus will come again, who say, "What happened to the promise that Jesus is coming again? From before the times of our ancestors, everything has remained the same since the world was first created" (2 Peter 3:4). What might you point to in the Bible and current events to make your case for the soon return of Christ?

- Spend some time reading John 8:2–12. Whom do you most identify with in this story? In what way do the words and actions of Jesus encourage you? In what way do they challenge you?

- Read Romans 11:17–20. Who was the apostle Paul talking about here? What do these verses mean to you personally?

- Is there someone in your life whom God has been prompting you to share the gospel with? Write down the name of that person here, and begin praying for him or her. Ask God for the right opportunity and timing to have that conversation.

Greg Laurie

Appendix A

How to Know God

You were created to know God in a personal way—to have a relationship with Him through His Son, Jesus Christ. So how do you start a relationship with God?

Realize That You Are a Sinner

No matter how good of a life we try to live, we still fall miserably short of being a good person. That is because we are all sinners. The Bible says that no one is good, not even one. (See Isaiah 53:6.) We cannot become who we are supposed to be without Jesus Christ.

Recognize That Jesus Christ Died on the Cross for You

The Bible tells us that "God showed his great love for us by sending Christ to die for us while we were still sinners" (Romans 5:8 NLT). This is the Good News, that God loves us so much that He sent His only Son to die in our place when we least deserved it.

Repent of Your Sin

The Bible says, "Now repent of your sins and turn to God, so that sins may be wiped away" (Acts 3:19 NLT). The word *repent* ans to change our direction in life. Instead of running from od, we can run toward Him.

Receive Jesus Christ into Your Life

Becoming a Christian is not merely believing some creed or going to church. It is having Christ Himself take residence in your life and heart. Jesus said, "Behold, I stand at the door and knock. If anyone hears My voice and opens the door, I will come in to him and dine with him, and he with Me" (Revelation 3:20).

If you would like to have a relationship with Christ, simply pray this prayer and mean it in your heart:

> "Dear Lord Jesus, I know I am a sinner. I believe You died for my sins. Right now, I turn from my sins and open the door of my heart and life. I confess You as my personal Lord and Savior. Thank You for saving me. Amen."

Let Us Know

If you have made a decision to follow Christ today, we at Harvest Ministries would like to hear from you and send you some materials to help you grow in your relationship with Him. Please contact us at www.harvest.org.

If you have an urgent need for immediate spiritual counseling, please call 951-687-6902 from 9:00 a.m. to 5:00 p.m. Pacific time.

Appendix B

Equipped to Evangelize

God is looking for men and women, boys and girls, who will say, "Lord, here I am. Send me." Will you share the gospel message with others? I hope so. You are commanded to do so (see Matthew 28:19–20), and the Lord will give you the power to do so. He will equip you to evangelize.

As you set out to share the good news with others, here are some important principles to remember.

Have a Burden for Those Who Don't Know the Lord

We could talk endlessly about the right way to answer certain difficult questions, how to start a conversation with a nonbeliever, or how to build a bridge to a person but all of that is useless if one essential is missing: you have to care about lost people.

Maybe there are certain people whom you're not comfortable talking to. Maybe they are of a different race than you, or maybe they are from a different neighborhood than you. Maybe their hair is a little different.

We have to look past hair color, tattoos, race, and age and realize that God has called us to take the gospel into all the world.

ryone needs to hear it. So the first thing we need to do is pray
t God would give us a burden for lost people.

Do you really care about people who don't know the Lord?
You have to start there.

Be Obedient

I have found that God generally leads one step at a time. When
the Lord asks you to take a step of obedience to Him, don't ask
for the big plan when you are not even willing to take the first
step. Just go.

Has God ever led you to speak to someone? Maybe it was
someone that you were burdened for. Maybe you found yourself
waking up in the middle of the night thinking about that person.
Maybe it was someone that you just saw somewhere and were
burdened by God's Spirit to talk to. You say, "I am not going,
Lord. You'd better get someone else."

He will. But He wanted to use you. That is why the Bible
says, "Preach the word! Be ready in season and out of season" (2
Timothy 4:2). Keep your spiritual antenna up and say, "Lord, I
am open. Is there someone You want me to talk to or something
You want me to do?" God can use you anywhere. Be on duty at
all times, and take that step of obedience.

Use Tact

What is tact? It has been defined as the intuitive knowledge of
saying the right thing at the right time. It is being sensitive to
the person you are speaking to, not editing the truth but having a
sense of what to say and when to say it.

A lot of Christians will say the stupidest things to nonbeliev ers, and then when they are rejected, they will respond, "Praise God! I am being persecuted for righteousness' sake."

No, they are being persecuted because they don't have any tact. They don't have any sensitivity.

I don't believe in shoving the gospel down anyone's throat. What I do believe in is throwing my hook in the water with a little bait. I will talk a little bit about Jesus. I will see what they do. I may say something like, "Jesus has really changed my life." If they run away screaming, that is not a good start.

They might say, "That is fine for you, but I don't want to talk about it."

Or, they might say, "What do you mean?"

I want to see if they will engage. I want to see if there is an interest first. I don't want to waste time talking to a person that doesn't want to hear it.

There is a place for telling a person there is a coming judgment. But let's try to establish a dialogue. Try to engage the other person first. Everyone's favorite subject is themselves. Ask them questions. Listen. Try to find common ground. And once you have made a connection, then share the gospel. Seek to build a bridge instead of burning one.

Know and Use the Scriptures

Any Christian worth his or her salt should be able to stand up at a moment's notice and clearly articulate the gospel message.

God said, "So shall My word be that goes forth from My mouth; it shall not return to Me void, but it shall accomplish

at I please, and it shall prosper in the thing for which I sent it"
saiah 55:11).

But what if the person you're speaking to doesn't believe the
Bible? Quote it anyway. God's Word is still alive and powerful.
When you quote the Bible, you can do so conversationally. You
don't have to scream it. You can share it in a loving, conversa-
tional way.

The Word of God is the Word of God, and it is alive and powerful whether a person believes it or not. I have quoted the Bible
when people have said they don't believe in it. But regardless
of what they say, I know it will stay with them. I have sown the
seed of God's Word in their lives. I water it with prayer and leave
the results in the hands of God.

Know and use the Word of God. Let people hear it.

Ask the Question

People need to understand that they have to make a decision
about Jesus. You have to close the deal. There is a time to sow
and a time to reap. We make a mistake when we try to reap when
it is not time. We have to wait on God's timing.

But there are also those who will share the gospel, love a person, build a bridge, and do all the right things, but they will never
ask the person, "Do you want to ask Jesus into your life?"

You say, "I can't do that. That is for the professionals to do. I
will bring them to church, and the pastor can do it."

You can do it too. You can lead that person in prayer. There is
no reason you can't. God can use you.

We are afraid of failure, but I also think some of us are afraid of success. I think we're afraid that people will say yes. We're afraid they will want to ask Jesus into their lives.

Go ahead and ask. And be prepared for success.

You can't close the deal, but God can. So be open to the leading of the Holy Spirit.

Appendix C

Helps for Small Groups

This book can be used for either individual or small group study. For those who are planning to discuss this book in a small group setting, the following helps are designed to assist you in maximizing your time together as a small group.

Have a Plan

Before your first meeting, determine how many weeks you'll spend going through this book and the accompanying video. How much time do you want to set aside for your group discussion? How much time do you want to spend watching the video? You'll also want to allow time for fellowship and prayer. Will you share a meal together, or will coffee or refreshments be served? Make these decisions in advance and then develop a timeline for your meeting prior to your first time together.

Set a Welcoming Tone

Some members of your small group will feel more comfortable in a group setting than others. Begin and end your group time in prayer. Establish some ground rules for the group from the begin-

, such as agreeing to keep what is shared in the group con-
ential and refraining from condemning or criticizing another
erson's comments.

Also consider starting your discussion time with an icebreak-
er question, something that everyone in the group can answer.
Icebreakers should help group members get to know each other
better, with questions like, "If you could travel back to any time
in history, when would it be?" or "What is your favorite dessert?"
or "Who was your favorite teacher, and why?"

Encourage Everyone to Participate

Some people are more naturally talkative than others, and that
can become especially evident in a small group setting. It's the
group leader's responsibility to encourage everyone to participate. It may require redirecting the discussion with a statement
like, "That's a great point, Bob. I also would be interested in
knowing Emily's thoughts on this. What do you think, Emily?"

For particularly shy or talkative group members, it may be
helpful to begin your discussion time with a statement such as,
"I'm looking forward to a great discussion tonight. I really want
to hear what everyone thinks about this topic."

Above all, ask God to give you His wisdom and discernment
to help you lead the discussion effectively.

Watch Your Time

The small group leader should have a watch, clock, or other
timekeeping device within view at all times during the meeting.
He or she is responsible for keeping the group on schedule and
respecting the group members' time.

Before the group meets, the leader should review the discussion questions. Decide how much time to realistically allow for each question and determine how many people can ideally participate within that timeframe.

The leader's objective should be to get through all the discussion questions planned for that meeting and to give everyone in the group an opportunity to participate.

And let us not neglect our meeting together, as some people do, but encourage one another, especially now that the day of his return is drawing near.

(Hebrews 10:25 NLT)

Notes

(Endnotes)

1. Pam Key, "Hagel: 'I Think We Are Seeing a New World Order,'" *Breitbart*, http://www.breitbart.com/video/2014/10/29/hagel-i-think-we-are-seeing-a-new-world-order/.

2. Anne Look, "2014 Sees Dramatic Uptick in Boko Haram Abductions," *Voice of America,* December 19, 2014, http://www.voanews.com/content/gumsuri-nigeria-might-be-site-of-another-mass-kidnapping-by-boko-haram/2566026.html.

3. Quoted in Tim LaHaye and Jerry B. Jenkins, *Are We Living in the End Times?* (Carol Stream, IL: Tyndale House Publishers, 1999), 47.

4. Judith Ingram, "Russia Signs Deal to Sell Iran Weapons" The Associated Press, October 2, 2001, http://www.seattlepi.com/national/article/Russia-signs-deal-to-sell-Iran-weapons-1067477.php.

5. Josh Rogin and Eli Lake, "Iran and North Korea: The Nuclear 'Axis of Resistance,'" *The Daily Beast*, March 31, 2014,

http://www.thedailybeast.com/articles/2014/01/31/iran-and-north-korea-the-nuclear-axis-of-resistance.html.

6. Reza Kahlili, "Iran General: Our Ultimate Goal Is the Destruction of America and Israel," *The Daily Caller,* January 5, 2014, http://dailycaller.com/2015/01/05/iran-general-our-ultimate-goal-is-the-destruction-of-america-and-israel/.

7. "Iran's Top Leader Spells Out Plan for the 'Elimination of Israel,' " World Jewish Congress, November 11, 2014, http://www.worldjewishcongress.org/en/news/15339/iran_s_top_leader_spells_out_plan_for_the_elimination_of_israel_.

8. "The Complete Transcript of Netanyahu's Address to Congress," *The Washington Post,* http://www.washingtonpost.com/blogs/post-politics/wp/2015/03/03/full-text-netanyahus-address-to-congress/.

9. Samuel Smith, "ISIS Rakes in $800 Million in Black Market Oil Sales Per Year, $2 Million Daily, Report Estimates," *The Christian Post*, October 22, 2014, http://www.christianpost.com/news/isis-rakes-in-800-million-in-black-market-oil-sales-per-year-2-million-daily-report-estimates-128439/.

10. Esther Tanquintic-Misa, "No Mercy: ISIS, Father Stones to Death Daughter for Alleged Adultery," *International Business Times*, October 22, 2014, http://au.ibtimes.com/articles/570345/20141022/mercy-isis-father-stones-death-daughter-adultery.htm#.VK6lrdh0zRY.

About the Author

Greg Laurie is the senior pastor of Harvest Christian Fellowship in Riverside and Orange County in California. Harvest is one of the largest churches in the United States and consistently ranks among the most influential churches in the country. He recently celebrated forty years as the senior pastor. In 1990, he began holding large-scale public evangelistic events called Harvest Crusades. More than five million people have attended Harvest events around the world, and more than 421,800 people have registered professions of faith through these outreaches.

He is the featured speaker of the nationally syndicated radio program *A New Beginning*, which is broadcast on more than seven hundred radio outlets worldwide. Along with his work at Harvest Ministries, he served as the 2013 honorary chairman of the National Day of Prayer and also serves on the board of directors of the Billy Graham Evangelistic Association.

He has authored over seventy books, including *As It Is in Heaven; Revelation: the Next Dimension; As I See It; Hope for Hurting Hearts; Married. Happily; Every Day with Jesus; Signs of the Times; Hope for America;* and many more.

He has been married to Cathe Laurie for forty years, and they have two sons, Christopher and Jonathan. Christopher went to be with the Lord in 2008. They also have five grandchildren.

Notes

Greg Laurie

Greg Laurie